Poetry
to Challenge
the Senses

To SHERYL
A GOOD FRIEND.

Donald Eling

Poetry to Challenge the Senses

Donald Elix

iUniverse

POETRY TO CHALLENGE THE SENSES

iUniverse books may be ordered through booksellers or by contacting:

iUniverse
1663 Liberty Drive
Bloomington, IN 47403
www.iuniverse.com
1-800-Authors (1-800-288-4677)

Because of the dynamic nature of the Internet, any web addresses or links contained in this book may have changed since publication and may no longer be valid. The views expressed in this work are solely those of the author and do not necessarily reflect the views of the publisher, and the publisher hereby disclaims any responsibility for them.

Any people depicted in stock imagery provided by Thinkstock are models, and such images are being used for illustrative purposes only. Certain stock imagery © Thinkstock.

ISBN: 978-1-4917-8935-3 (sc)
ISBN: 978-1-4917-8936-0 (e)

Library of Congress Control Number: 2016902257

Print information available on the last page.

iUniverse rev. date: 04/06/2016

Contents

Standing in My Mind's Eye

I move to dissociate myself from those things I encounter, from those people I would encounter.

My world expands with each passing thought, each one flowing and akin to the prior, floating in endless diversion to kindle the fire that will burn.

Gentle the breeze that fans the lazy columns of smoke rising to the endless heavens, reaching for life as the embryo at birth.

What more is living than death—and death to new life—the seasons passing one to the next and returning true, each in its cycle starting?

I live fully within, and I reach toward what is without, when standing in my mind's eye.

Torment in Absence

The pain is felt in my inner soul;
The grief, unexplainable.
My mind cries out to the limits of eternity.

Darkness, as if light years away,
Comes calling to my consciousness.
Nonwaking torment is cradled, as
If demonic, in heavenly auras.

As future redwoods in twin plantings
Must be joined with their kind,
They scream at the jacks who would
Violate them to use them as tools of insidiousness, tools of the human kind.

Alas, the redwoods are toppled as the Creator
Watches in dismay,
Awaiting the appointed time …

Escape to Imagination

The sun rides low, far to the south and west.
  The barren landscape embraces the last warming rays.
It's purely desolate here, especially close to sunset—
A place not welcoming to us, but here we are nonetheless.

We've been here. We've dreamed of walking in the crisp evening air.
We've enjoyed the solitude of this wholesome winter scene;
Yes, we've even loved every waning second.

It's been invigorating to our senses.
The snow crunching over the concrete earth and
The smell of smoke from chimneys close by
Reassure us when we've lost ourselves to the moment.

But something clouds our vision now,
Nagging at our minds as if to snap our warmest dreams.
It's distant, yet it gains with ever-increasing speed as fleeting thoughts race
away from us.
Now our cabin rounds into view, a thin wisp
Of smoke rising from the stack to touch the azure sky.
Within those walls we know that the heat from
The redbrick hearth will warm away our cares.

We now sit and thaw, as outside the elements
Make their nocturnal change, bringing depths of chill.
It feels good, the log fire, as we wrap ourselves
In its secure embrace.

It's fading now; it leaves our thoughts.
Why? What good reason? It was so clear and made such good atmosphere.
Ah! Now we see. Our thoughts propel us across
Boundaries of imagination to our dreamy season.

These things were real to us. They kept us going
In times of stress.
We knew that place, and we knew that we must return to perpetuate our
dream.
Whether or not we live for this, it is urgent to us.

For us, we live in the *dolor* of eight to five.
We lust for the time to be ourselves in times
And at places lost to others.
This is what drives us beyond acquiring material objects
To accomplish deeds of individual esteem.
(The best is still to come.)
For this we yearn. We build for it
So we can leave and live beyond,
In memories of fleeting thoughts.
This is our escape to imagination.

Dirt

Many ways is dirt recalled,
Depending on the need.
To some it's good old mother earth, for
Planting seed and reaping crops: good old sod.

To others it's filthy, grimy stuff. It's dust
To eat behind a cattle herd and for the cows to choke their
Parched throats on.

Now and then it's therapy, to those who work
In the asphalt and concrete city: honest magical turf.

To all of us it's one thing or another,
But necessary it is, to all of us.

The ways to use it are many, but to all of us dirt has a use:
To spring forth flowers and lush green grass;
To grow the fruit and nut trees and the vegetable vines;
To harbor sailing ships at water's end or
Land's end, as you choose;
To cover it for a dwelling place or to uncover it
For children's play;
To mine the minerals and the metals to make
Life easier.

Good old dirt has it all, if used in every way.
It's beautiful, it's ugly, it's peaceful and restful.
It's violent and torturous.
It's there for us to use as best we can.

Dedicated to You

You know the sun will always shine,
  Though you may sometimes filter it.
You think the rain will never stop.
We know it does. We've seen it stop.

So now the clouds filter out the sun,
And rain falls constantly.
The sun's still there; the rain will stop.
But what of a love we once shared?

Have clouds cast shadows to block the sun?
Does rain now cease to stop?
These things we know to be untrue.
By creation they were set to last for eternity.

I'd like to think as our Creator did
When he set the rules for our elements.
That our love may filter through the clouds,
However dense they are, and that rain will only
Make it grow as years pass, moving on and on.

For without you and me to make it so,
Our love does not exist.
But by our being and knowing it,
It exists for time indefinite.

So come, run through the clouds and rain with me.

The Simple Life

Such a simple chore was his
    In a different time, in a peaceful town.
He was the solid, steadfast symbol of the simple life.
Every dusk, he made his rounds to brighten the
Lives of all who saw and knew him.
He was the old town lamplighter.

Past houses and huts with rooves of thatch,
Along the fabled streets of cobblestone,
With nary a hitch and not a minute's tarry,
He knew his work well and went about it.
Remembering frosty nights when fog was all about,
He made his rounds, the old lamplighter.

In quaint old villages where pubs abound,
You still hear murmurs of times long ago,
Of when horses brought the milkman to your door.
Faithful was he to wake the sleepiest
With the clink of bottles, pints full of milk.
Those days started and ended with him, the old lamplighter.

The butcher, the chemist, the smithies too,
The shoemaker, the cobbler, the printer—and still—
The farmer, the shepherd, the salt of the earth,
Plowed furrows, made products, and carried them forth
To sell in the markets, which closed at dusk
So the streets could be lit by the lamplighter.

Quiet Village

The mists of gloom sift through the trees
  And roll through streets deserted.
Stillness lingers here now,
And peace wraps roundabout.

The fog and cold of night,
I find it so refreshing.
No thoughts of danger came to me
While I was passing through the mists.

It also seemed that one could wander
Most anywhere he chose.
Day or night no difference made;
Alone, one tarried safe.

How wonderful the friendships made
With cheery people there.
That tiny English village,
We lived in and loved that place.

Appreciation for the things that made life so much better
Came only when we left that place and moved to where it wasn't.

"There'll always be an England"
Echoes over there.

I pray that the ones who declare thus are right,
For if they are, we'll go back some day.

Mirrors of Emotion

You're lovely in the early morn;
    You're lovely late at night.
You're lovely when the weather's good.
You're always lovely when you smile.

But when the clouds roll overhead
And the sky gets dark and gray,
Your smile flees into the leaden sky and
Your mood becomes a thunderhead.

I wish that you could see some good
In rain and a cloudy sky.
To moderate your temperament,
Your sunny smile returns.

You see, I love you, rain or shine—
That's why I reflect your moods.
To rise above and change your moods,
For me, is a most fearsome task.

You see, I'll try and try and try,
Because I love you so.
For life without you either way
Means little to me now.

Pondering in Limbo

Sitting here alone and quiet, I find my mind in turmoil still.
It's often said that we regret the words and deeds we say and do in haste.

So soon the dusk, so long the dawn;
How long the dark does tarry.
Be for me as I am for you;
Let naught tear us asunder.

If I find words to make the future brighter,
I'll write them till my eyes don't see.
But actions are to me more dear than eyes to see the words.
I spoke in haste!

My tongue cannot retrieve the waste;
It can but utter more.
My heart beats with my head
And wishes to be forgiven for
The utterances foolishly made.

These words were lovingly thought in quietness!

Blue Sunset

The sun is fading now and dusk is settling in.
      Wisps of strata float aimlessly toward the darkening horizon.
Majestic firs nestle in ebony satin cloaks for nocturnal hiding.
Patches of brilliant blue embrace the last rays of day.

The evening sky now trades its rays of day
For a cloak of dark.
Now, after sunset,
Brightness fades into thousands of subdued,
Nameless, incandescent, twinkling lights
Against a blanket of black, which engulfs
The earth as far as the mind can fathom—
Not long removed from another blue sunrise.

A Place for Me

A place to go, to be alone,
        To put the thoughts at peace,
To straighten out a troubled mind—
A place where humans seldom stray.
To have a place all to yourself,
To let your mind roam free.
To breathe in nature's loving best.
Left alone to age and rest.
I found this place in one small corner.
It could not hide from me,
For it was the place I had been seeking
Since childhood days long past.
A waterfall to please the ear.
A silken pond behind
Made beautiful by moonlight beams.
Often I would wander
Away from noise and worry,
Alone to feast and drink
Of land and scenery steeped
In history, ages past,
As humankind passed on.
It is across an ocean of dreams and memories.
For quiet solitude, withdrawn
In mind, is sweet release.

Ode to Molly

'Twas a lonely night when first we met.
        You were a friend's companion at the time.
But not long after, as meetings came and went,
We came to know each other so;
Soon we knew we'd have to share time together,
As it were.
From the first time we met, you wanted to know more of me, and I of you.
As if fated, we explored togetherness and found a beautiful relationship.

As I recall those happy months,
I am sure that we knew 'twas more than just a fancy.
The walks upon the peaceful hills
To our precious spot to see the view—
We gloried in our own love building,
For we alone enjoyed our world.
O the feelings that two people gain
From sharing in each other's lives,
Loving those close around us,
Finding time to transfer the beauty of our newfound
Sharing in order to share with them.

When I recall the timeless moments
We shared just walking with each other,
I remember that it mattered not of material things,
As we had each other to embrace.
To all our friends it must have shown,
For our love was most exalted and we knew it to be so.
To us it happened, as I reflect.
How beautiful it was!

Soon there will be a time for us
To share alone in timeless moments,
To live again the best of times,
A new world and tides to wash, to ebb and flow,
Our love eternal.
To take or leave the words outside.
This time is ours alone to bask in splendor.

Molly, you gave me life and, truly so,
Someone to love, as you loved me.
The trying times were not so bad.
You shared those, too, for love of me.
No longer did I just exist.
There's more to life, we both have learned.
And when it's time for life eternal,
I know we'll both start it anew.
For all that's known as love to me
Is an ode to Molly.

One for All

We stand alone except for one
    We all can surely lean on.
When times are tough, we learn a lot;
When not so tough, we tend to stray.

There are those who lean behind closed doors
And those who openly depend on God.
He understands in either case, as
He's always there when needed.

There'll come a time, and very soon,
When those who lean on him will know.
He's the only one who helps,
And he too has a price.

Is love's and truth's and kindness's cost
Too much for us to pay,
For him and for each other,
Throughout eternity?

For what he has in store for us,
We can only guess.
Rest assured, we'll prosper from it.
This it has been promised.

Mother of Mine

Mother of mine, you gave me life.
    You nurtured me, loved me, and made me whole.
You gave me your smile. It shined on me
Like the sun on a delicate flower.
You give me hugs; they surrounded me and protected me like the bark of
a tree.
You gave me nourishment and wisdom as I grew.
You encouraged me and cheered for me even when I fell down.

Mother of mine, mother of mine.
When you got older, and I did too, the smile still shined,
The hugs were still given, the nourishment was still there, and still the
wisdom grew.

Mother of mine, mother of mine.
You taught me much, and it made you tired.
I gave back what I could. You smiled a knowing smile and talked of good
old days.

Mother of mine, mother of mine.
Now you've gone to rest, to peace, to your lasting home.
God bless you, mother of mine!

Definition of a Love

A friend in need is a friend indeed,
A person to support in good times as well as in bad,
A partner who senses actions before they start,
A lover for all seasons,

One who knows solitude as well as gathering,
One who feels with the heart and thinks with the head,
One who loves the delicate scent of a spring flower,
One who may be solemn and then spring momentously
Into childish laughter.

A love is a deep abiding respect for living and feeling through tender emotion.
A love may share moments that span infinite
Time and space before returning to earth.
A love is one that fears neither birth nor death,
As neither is final.
Most of all, a love is caring and showing deep devotion to God's creation
through all that is living.

My love is a love, and my heart speaks to her as a Valentine.

Beside the Sea

It's peaceful here beside the sea,
    Where waves crash on the sand incessantly.
The sand just sifts and throws them back
To echo in the mist.

The ghostly moon throws shadows faintly
Upon the phosphorescent crests,
Silently weaving endless thought
As to and fro it pulls the mind.

Somewhere there, on the vast expanse,
A foghorn wails its melancholy sound.
The steady flashing beacon from the point
Warns of danger from its lofty crown.

The sounds, the salt spray, and the mist
Lend themselves to magic spells.
The world turns around this shore,
Where time stands still and senses sway.

I think I'll just stay here
And dream, and rest, beside the sea.

The Old-Town Place

A peaceful place to have a cup,
    To sit and rest and to gather thoughts.
To dream a little far from it.
To me it means a lot,
This friendly old-town place.

I've worked here and talked here.
I've always been at ease.
A little corner just for me—
I need it now and then.

When troubles pile as high as the sky,
I know a place to go
To rest a while and gather peace:
Here at the old-town place.

There's lots of room to stretch your legs—
Maybe stretch your mind a bit.
Yet it's as cozy as a country store
Warmed by a wood-burning stove.

Always a haven; never a boredom.
I'm often glad it's here.
I look forward to passing many more hours
In this friendly old-town place.

Garden of Eden

We languish in the city streets,
    Crushed by those who are here with us.
They come here by the score,
From off the yoke and truss.

It's here that business does abound,
Spreads the wealth among those who are prepared.
But for those who are unfortunate,
No wealth is to be found.

Let freedom ring for all those who toil.
Let freedom ring for those who work and want.

The redbrick halls lined with goods
Await their every fancy.
They bid them forth, extract their measure,
Cater to their every pleasure.

They come and go. They fritter so,
Belying all their treasure,
While on the sod the workers plod
To draw their scanty wages.

Let freedom ring. For all those who have it, get it.
Let freedom ring for those who are pushing plows.
Let freedom ring. They all have got what they want for now.

Soul Season

The sun sets sooner now with the next season coming.
Our love goes further into the setting sun.
The season dictates its own romance with falling leaves and
Cool, crisp air, whispering, *Soon*
Will come the snow.

Magenta shades of dusk, closer now to homeward bound.
Rosy-cheeked children frolic in the last rays of light.
What more to do? What more to see? Has it not happened all before?
Season after season, year after year, still we seek the cycle to continue.

For after all, who knows the depths of humankind's torment?
Who knows the cold of people's sorrow, longing, wanting, and needing,
all for love?

What mad rationale dictates the fate of our lives?
Who decides and then punishes himself severely?
How do we beckon the values of the past
To shape ethereal images of our future?

The spans that gulf these troubled waters
Fade into abaxial images toward the mass.
Autumn falls in splashing splendor,
A new start.
Come forth, you cleansing snows of winter.

The Piper

The pipers echo through the glen.
　　　The melancholy notes whisper on a feather,
Sending light currents of air into the heather below.

The chords remind me of you
And of bygone days of standing together
Alone, except that the earth and the heavens served as the stage for our
solitude.

We knew and know of each other, have
Thoughts that are born of sharing and then are shared without,
In need of spoken word.

The piper perched upon his crag knows of such devotion.
Freezing mist may bear witness to those of stout character.

As our senses hear and feel and see such things
As may not be again,
We hold and possess these precious slots in time
As treasures all our own.

No others grasp them 'cept we alone.
Infinitely ours, these moments shared.
Our piper stands the test of time.
He needs not words to persevere.

Timbers

*T*he leather does fly at the sound of a whistle,
From volley to header, a try at the net.
The pitch rings with shots aimed like a missile.
The home team is here; continue to whistle.

They've come from afar, as well as from close by.
They're here to do well or at least give it a try.
You'll know by the roar of the crowd here today that
The Timbers are playing. Let's hope things go their way.

From midfield to forward to midfield again,
The ball is booted and headed to win.
The keeper is moving from side to side
As fullbacks roam near, protecting his hide.

From one end to the other and back again,
They tirelessly run on to parry a thrust.
Trapping and shooting or passing is a must
For swaying the action, to try for the win.

Excitement runs thick as the action continues,
Forever moving from end to end.
Trying hard to please all the folks in the venue,
The Timbers roll on, the team that Portland defends.

Individual Pleasure

When I sit down to meditate,
    Thoughts race through my mind.
They seem to be of the kind
I'd like to keep of late.

So I put them on paper,
To come back and read at times.
They need not be the kind that rhyme,
Because they sometimes taper.

They are meant to be put in print,
To be shared for a profit.
They are not meant to be scoffed at
But to communicate what I meant.

To me they are a good release
When trying times obscure.
To write them down, to me it occurs,
Brings me some peace.

If it did not bring me pleasure,
Then to me it would be work.
Therein the danger would surely lurk.
It proves to me my measure.

Since it does come naturally
And falls into place so well,
I often sit in thoughts to dwell on
And write casually.

Make Time for Dreams

When I dream, I'm young, I'm strong in spirit.
Dreaming allows me time to resolve myself to achieving the goals I must attain.
To dream is to plan for the impossible,
The struggle to attain great personal goals.

As I live and learn, I must continue to dream.
To me this is living in its best sense.
To accomplish feats once dreamed about is the
Point of dreaming at all.

Yes, dreaming may be an escape. All of us escape grim realities at times.
Franklin dreamed of great inventions; Columbus, of discovering a new land.
King dreamed of the races living in peace. Sabin dreamed of curing polio and is still dreaming.
Our pioneer ancestors dreamed of living their lives in peace and prosperity.
Their plan worked well for many years.

I can be as great as any of them if I make reality of my dreams.
In a personal way, to make a wish, dream about it, work hard for it,
And then see it happen is the ultimate boost for an individual's ego.

When you have time, dream also.
Sometimes you must make time to dream, for it is the start of most good things that happen.

The Greatest Triumph

The greatest triumph in life is for a person to become mentally
strong enough to rise above
Everyday trials so that he or she may achieve, both physically and mentally,
to his or her greatest
Allowable degree.

If this is done,
Most individuals find their achievements to be
Far beyond their wildest imagining.

If, when your trials appear insurmountable,
You will recall these words, you may become a mirror,
Reflecting the potential of others while exploiting your own ability to
achieve.

Printed in the United States
By Bookmasters